This book is dedicated to you.

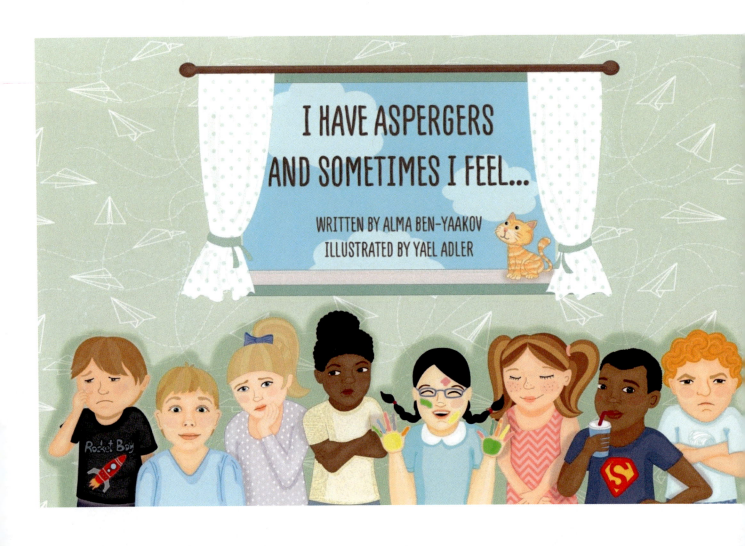

I Have Aspergers and Sometimes I Feel...

Second Edition (with new cover)

Alma Ben-Yaakov

Tango Golf Digital, LLC

Palo Alto, California

Tango Golf Digital, LLC, Palo Alto, California

© 2016 by Alma Ben-Yaakov
All rights reserved.

ISBN-13: 978-1539514732
ISBN-10: 1539514730

eBook ISBN: 978-0-692-73208-3

About This Book

More and more children are being diagnosed with autism spectrum disorders. Asperger syndrome is one of several previously separate subtypes of autism that were folded into the single diagnosis autism spectrum disorder (ASD). [1] Children with ASD need repeated encouragement and assistance to identify and name the feelings that they experience. This book presents an opportunity for parents and caregivers to open conversations with children with Aspergers or ASD, or any child who might benefit.

[1] https://www.autismspeaks.org/what-autism/asperger-syndrome (from May 31, 2016)

I have Aspergers and sometimes I feel *angry*.

I feel *angry* when I don't know how to play with other kids.

I have Aspergers and sometimes I feel *amazed*.

I feel *amazed* when I solve a computer problem that no one else could.

I have Aspergers and sometimes I feel *jealous*.

I feel *jealous* when I see how easy it is for my brother to make friends.

I have Aspergers and sometimes I feel *proud*.

I feel *proud* when I talk to the cashier in the coffee shop all by myself.

I have Aspergers and sometimes I feel *worried*.

I feel *worried* when I think about what will happen when I grow up.

I have Aspergers and sometimes I feel *happy*.

I feel *happy* when I play with a new kid.

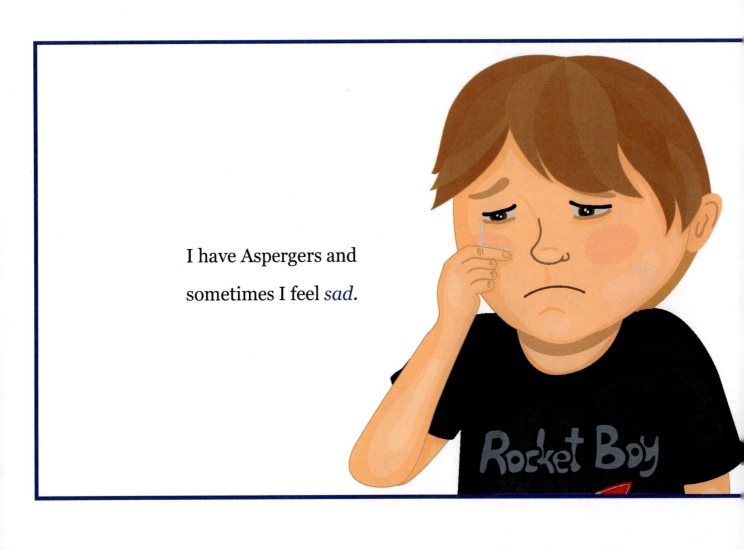

I have Aspergers and sometimes I feel *sad*.

I feel *sad* when I don't know how to control my anger.

I have Aspergers and

I feel *loved*.

My family *loves* me just the way I am.

About the Author

Alma Ben-Yaakov is a mother and an educator with many years of experience. Her focus on educating young children, some with special challenges, led her to study more about autism spectrum disorder, including Aspergers. Alma lives in Texas with her husband and two children. This is her first book.

email: alma@tangogolfdigital.com
facebook: https:// www.facebook.com/TangoGolfDigital

About the Illustrator

Yael Adler began her studies in Industrial Design but by chance and with a lot of luck found her way to graphics and illustration, a profession which she adores. Yael lives in Israel.

email: yaelnathan@gmail.com
facebook: https://www.facebook.com/yaeladler26

Made in the USA
Las Vegas, NV
03 January 2023

64900544R00017